How to
Paint on Silk

Edited by Pam Dawson

Search Press

Introduction

It is the caterpillar of the silkworm moth, which produces that most noble of textile fibres – silk. It feeds on mulberry leaves and spins itself a cocoon which can be made up of threads as much as 3,000 metres or nearly 10,000 feet in length–very fine, elastic, and strong.

Silkworms have been kept in China for over 4,000 years. The penalty for smuggling them out of the country used to be death. As a result, only the finished fabrics reached the rest of the world, along the famous 'Silk route' to Europe. In the sixth century monks are believed to have hidden the eggs of the silkworm in their staffs and smuggled them to Byzantium. Silkworms also reached India and Japan. In Italy silk was produced in the twelfth century, in France the first silk was woven in Lyons in the sixteenth century. Painting on silk, which by then was highly developed in the Far East, was now taken up widely in France, and French style and techniques came to influence the rest of the Western world. Soon, however, it became forgotten, until early in the present century when it was rediscovered in southern France and Brittany.

Nowadays even the amateur can achieve excellent results with modern silk paints. The brilliance of these silk paints and the luxuriousness of the smooth, rich silk fabrics is an irresistible combination.

Two attributes are essential for the silk artist: not simply drawing skills and colour sense, as might be expected, so much as patience and diligence. With these the basic skills of silk painting are quickly learned, for the craft is not as difficult to work as it at first appears to be.

Is it an expensive hobby? It is certainly not cheap for of course, silk is a precious material. Nor will your first product be a masterpiece! So start by practising with small-scale items. These will quickly reveal, however, what a wealth of possibilities there is in silk painting, for no other material or technique produces such luminous colours, and such experiments can lead on to magical results.

It is beyond the scope of this book to describe all the possible variations, but in the opening section of the book the basic techniques are explained and the few basic tools and materials that are necessary are described. In the rest of the book the main emphasis is on the objects you can make – cushions, pictures, scarves, dresses, and other, smaller items.

Whether one is an experienced artist working in a studio, or a beginner painting on the kitchen table or in the garden, it is possible to learn and to enjoy. The experienced artist will draw inspiration for his designs from the world around him; the beginner, on the other hand, will find suggestions in this book for drawings that are ideal for teaching technique. It is also best to begin with small items, such as a bag or greetings card, and then to advance from these to the more ambitious and fashionable projects which are illustrated in this book.

Above: this striking design uses simple techniques and brilliant colours to achieve the maximum effect. The completed painting would make a suitable picture, scarf or cushion cover.

How to begin

Once you have mastered the basic techniques, this exciting craft can be used to produce original and luxurious items at relatively low costs. Be realistic about your first attempt, however, and begin with something small enough in area and simple enough in design to guarantee successful results. As your confidence grows, you will feel able to tackle some of the more complicated designs featured in this book.

Before attempting to paint on silk it is important to understand that you will never be able to reproduce an exact replica of any illustration. Silk is a natural fibre and, much like wool, varies in quality and texture. Paints may also vary from one manufacturer to another in texture and colour. Another point to bear in mind is that an original design may have been drawn free-hand, without any clear lines of reference, so is a 'one-off'. These factors, however, are what make this craft so fascinating, as you will always produce your own unique design.

Make sure you have everything you will require to hand before beginning any project. You will need to work quickly to achieve satisfactory results and if you have to break off in the middle of an operation because you have forgotten to buy a brush fine enough to paint small areas, the whole process could be ruined.

You need not make any vast initial outlay on tools or materials. Scraps of silk can be found on most remnant counters at prices to suit all purses.

Tools

The basic tools needed for silk painting are easily obtainable in art and craft shops or by mail order from specialist suppliers. Some tools can even be made at home. The beginner's kit should contain the following:

1 wooden frame
Silk fabric
Silk paints in two or three colours
Brushes
Pins
Gutta, or blocking agent
Salt
Thinner and fixing agent–as recommended by the manufacturer of the range of paints used
A colour chart–helpful in deciding on a colour scheme (see page 7)

Frames

Silk can only be painted successfully if the fabric is evenly stretched and freely suspended. Purpose-made flat wooden frames–which can be adjusted and extended with additional pieces of wood from picture postcard size to 120 in × 56 in (300 cm × 140 cm)–are on the market (see page 5). These frames can also be readjusted during painting. For the beginner a fixed frame made from four pieces of wood screwed together with four metal angle pieces is quite sufficient; but since it is not adjustable this has to be made to the correct size of the fabric to be painted. For instance: for square scarves, which use silk 40 in (100 cm) wide, the inner opening should be 38 in × 38 in (95 cm × 95 cm).

Before any silk is stretched on to the frame, cover the frame with wide Sellotape, so that it can be easily wiped clean with a damp cloth and no remains of paint from previous work will spoil a new piece of silk.

Small items–such as greetings cards (see page 18) may be stretched in an embroidery or Tambour frame, or placed over a jam jar or rimmed glass dish and held in place with a strong elastic band or cord.

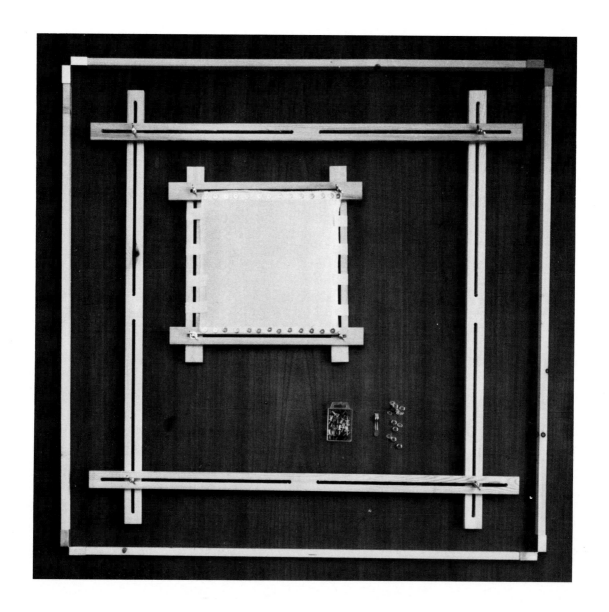

Silk fabrics

There are many different silk fabrics on the market, from very shiny and transparent organza to dull, heavily textured wild silks and noil. Not all of these are suitable for every silk painting technique, indeed they will impose their own very different characteristics on to the design. Heavily textured silks will not, for example, take the dyes evenly. They will also tend to encourage 'bridge-building' when 'gutta' is applied (see gutta-technique, page 11) – and this will later allow the colours to break through a gutta line and run into each other. Very thick silks may need a gutta application on both sides.

Whatever type of fabric is chosen for your first project, only unbleached white, or pale cream, give backgrounds that will produce clear, brilliant colours as the paints are applied. An important point to remember is that white is a hue not represented in any range of silk paints, so the white background of the fabric is used in many designs to highlight an area, or to define outlines between blocks of colours.

As you progress in expertise, you may wish to experiment to see what effects can be obtained by using pale, pastel backgrounds. In this event, the background colour chosen will be the palest shade in a design and you will not be able to introduce any white. The background colour will also have an effect on the paints you use and it will be difficult to visualize the finished colouring of a design.

All materials have to be washed, before they can be used for painting, in order to remove any traces of dressing and grease. Wash by hand in hand-warm water with a gentle detergent. Rinse well, roll the fabric into a towel and, when it is still damp, iron with a warm iron.

Fine silks can be torn, but thicker fabrics have to be cut carefully along the grain.

Silk paints

Silk paints divide into two groups: alcohol-based paints, and water-based paints. Both types are marketed as a watery liquid and are applied in the same way, but thinning and fixing methods differ.

Water-based paints are thinned down with water to lighten their tones, and they are made permanent or 'fixed' by simply ironing the painted silk with an electric iron (see page 16).

Alcohol-based paints can also be thinned down with water, but a special thinning liquid will ensure a more even application. The fixing process is more complicated as it involves steaming (see page 16), but the end result tends to be more brilliant.

Some firms offer a brush-on fixative (see page 16). Because of the different methods of fixing and thinning it is important to read and follow carefully the manufacturer's instructions on the paint bottles.

Colours of the same range can be freely mixed to create new colours or different tones and shades (see overleaf). Colours of different ranges or from different manufacturers should never, however, be mixed. Also it is not advisable to use gutta or fixatives of one make in combination with paints of another make. Some paints are offered in a thicker consistency. These will not run when painted on to dry silk, and they may be mixed with thinner paints of the same range.

Simple colour mixing

Most manufacturers offer many colours in each range of silk paints, but as they can be freely mixed within each range, two or three well-chosen colours will create quite a full palette.

The colour triangle (opposite) shows the three 'primary' colours as: cadmium yellow (1) magenta (5) light blue (9).

Colour chart

1 cadmium yellow
2 orange
3 scarlet
4 carmine
5 magenta
6 purple
7 violet
8 ultramarine
9 light blue
10 turquoise (cyan)
11 medium-green
12 yellow-green

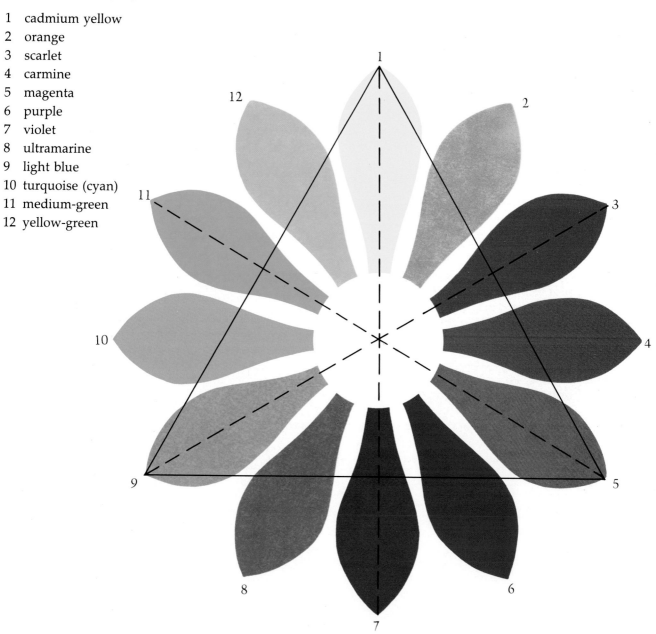

When two of these 'primary' colours are mixed in equal quantities 'secondary' colours are created:

cadmium yellow + magenta = orange (2)
magenta + light blue = violet (7)
light blue + cadmium yellow = medium green (11)

A group of six 'second-order secondary' colours is created when a 'primary' colour is mixed with a 'secondary' colour.

cadmium yellow + scarlet = orange (2)
scarlet + magenta = carmine (4)
magenta + violet = purple (6)
violet + light blue = ultramarine (8)
light blue + medium green = cyan (10)
medium green + cadmium yellow = yellow green (12)

The natural or white colour of the silk fabric is the lightest tone available. Any area meant to stay in the background colour is painted with a blocking agent or 'gutta' (see 'Gutta technique', page 11)

Each colour can be lightened to the gentlest pastel tones by adding more water, or a thinning agent if so recommended by the manufacturers. Black diluted will turn to greys.

Watch point:
When painting larger areas with mixed or thinned paint, make sure to mix enough paint, as it is not always possible to repeat a tone or colour accurately by mixing. It is better to have too much than too little. Mixed paints can be kept almost indefinitely in glass jars with well-fitting lids and preferably in the dark. Shake or stir them well before use, as the pigment sometimes settles on the bottom of the jar.

Brushes

The most suitable brushes to use are watercolour brushes which come to a fine point. They carry a lot of paint and give it out slowly and evenly.

At the top of the range are the Japanese brushes but,

for the beginner, brushes of student quality, thick, medium and fine, are quite adequate.

It is best to use one brush for each colour, so as not to contaminate their hue with any possible remaining paint of a different colour.

Brushes are not cheap and the better they are looked after the longer they will last. After use, wash them out in lukewarm water, shape them to a good straight point and keep them upside down in a glass or a jug.

Large areas of background can be painted with bunches of cotton wool or a sponge.

Watch point:
Either use a clothes-peg to hold the cotton wool or sponge or wear rubber gloves to protect your hands. If a fixative agent is used, it is best applied with a wide, stiff brush and by using long even strokes.

Pins

To hold the silk fabric to the frame, stainless steel pins must be used. Map-, decor-, or drawing-pins are suitable, but there are also available in art and craft shops special three-pronged flat-headed tacks.

Gutta, or blocking agent

A blocking agent or 'gutta' is used in the gutta-technique of silk painting (see page 11), or to block out areas of the design which the artist wants to keep in the colour of the silk fabric.

Watch point:
Always use the blocking agent that is recommended by the manufacturer of the range of paints you are using. Sometimes it is marketed in bottles which can be fitted with nozzles of varying sizes, sometimes the bottles themselves are pointed. There are also special gutta dispensers on offer.

The most commonly used blocking agent is transparent. When the silk is washed after the paints have been fixed, the transparent gutta will disappear and only leave a line of the original colour of the fabric, usually natural or white.

Gutta is also available in black, silver and gold. This means that the colour lines of the design drawn with gutta will remain black, silver or gold. This can look very decorative and festive, but it will not stand up to frequent washing and ironing. Dry cleaning may remove the gold and silver gutta.

Watch point:
Protect your ironing board with a cloth, as sometimes the gold and silver will transfer itself to the board during ironing.

Salt

To create the marbled effect of the salt technique (see page 14) special salt can be bought from silk suppliers, but any cooking salt can be used, fine or coarse. Salt crystals, as used in water softeners, are also suitable. Coarse salt will produce larger-scale effects, and finer salts finer marbling.

Dressing the frame

With the frame covered with Sellotape, and the silk washed and ironed as described in previous sections (page 4), we are now ready to begin.

The silk needs to be stretched evenly over the frame and as tightly as on a drum. Start at the bottom edge of the frame with the right side of the silk uppermost. Line it up with a straight edge of the fabric, and hold the silk in place with one pin or tack in each corner

pulling the silk as tight as possible. Next, pin down the centre, then the centres to the right and to the left all along the bottom edge, until the intervals are no bigger than 2 in (5 cm). Work in the same way along the opposite edge and finally along the two sides. Adjustable frames can now be tightened a final time.

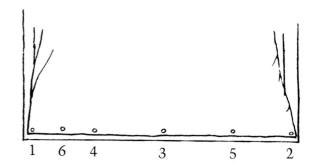

This shows the position of the pins, when attaching the silk to the frame.

Watch point:
During pinning no pleats, stretch marks or wavy lines should appear on the silk fabric. To make sure that the silk is freely suspended and not anywhere in touch with the table, it is best to lift the frame off the table by supporting all four corners with four tins or small boxes. (The cardboard insides of wide Sellotape rolls are ideal.)

9

Techniques

Gutta technique

Gutta-technique is sometimes referred to as blocking-technique, or resist-technique, or outline-technique.

First, either sketch the design lightly on to the silk or place a suitable drawing directly behind the fabric. With fine silks the outlines ought to show through sufficiently to be copied.

Fit the gutta-bottle directly with a nozzle of suitable width or transfer the gutta to a special dispenser. Now copy the outlines of the design with gutta on to the silk and leave it to dry according to the manufacturer's instructions. This can take anything from 10-30 minutes. These gutta lines will stop the paints from running into each other. If transparent gutta is used, a line in the original colour of the silk fabric will remain. If a coloured gutta is used the line drawing will appear in the colour of the gutta used. The designs best suited for this technique have long flowing lines without too many stops and starts, for the gutta has the tendency to start and finish with a blob.

Watch point:
Wipe the nozzle with a tissue before each new start.

Do not draw too slowly but with an even flow. Hold the frame against the light to check that the gutta lines are uninterrupted and have sunk into the silk properly everywhere, and make sure that all lines are closed. With very knobbly silks there is that tendency to 'bridge-building' where the gutta is trailing and not in touch with the silk. Mend any gaps and again leave it all to dry.

When the gutta is dry, the paints can be applied to the gutta-surrounded areas. Start in the middle of a 'field' with a full brush but paint only to near the edge of the 'field'. The colour will spread out to the gutta lines. Apply first the light colours of the design. Should there be a leak through an unnoticed gap in the gutta line this can be mended and covered up later with the darker colours.

Leave the painting to dry for a few hours. Next, the colours will have to be made permanent or 'fixed' according to the manufacturer's instructions (see page 16).

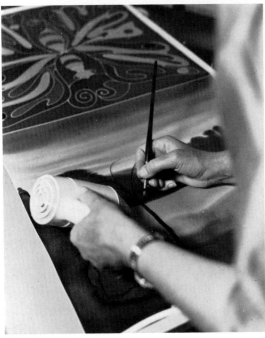

Watercolour technique

With the watercolour technique no gutta is used to keep the colours apart; instead they are allowed to flow into each other. This technique is particularly suitable for landscapes (see opposite).

To stop the silk from drying out too quickly during painting, the whole fabric is brushed with either water or a thinner, according to the manufacturer's instructions, then paints are applied briskly on to the wet silk. Start with the lighter colours of the sky, working downwards to the medium tones of the middle distance and the darker tones of the foreground at the bottom edge of the frame.

Details can now be added by drawing some more horizontal lines on to the wet background or brushing in shapes for trees and bushes. The colours will fuse into each other with no hard lines or contours.

Watch point:
Start with small blots of paint, as they will spread and grow.

After the background is dry more details can be added. Brush strokes with only water or thinner will break up the even colouring, irregular watermarks will appear, and also lighter areas with darker edges and lines not unlike distant mountain ranges.

Leave this to dry again, before adding more precise details like tree trunks or grasses in the foreground. Either use thickened paint, which does not run on a dry background, or use an ordinary electric hair-dryer. Hold the paintbrush in one hand, the hair-dryer, on a medium setting, in the other, and, immediately after applying the paint, blow it dry so that it has no chance to spread.

Finally, leave everything to dry thoroughly for a few hours before fixing the colours according to manufacturer's instructions (see page 16).

Above: landscape in watercolour technique.

Salt technique

Both the gutta and watercolour techniques of silk painting may be combined with each other, and either or both may be combined with the salt technique.

Since salt attracts water, if there is colour pigment suspended in the water it will be attracted by salt as well. So if kernels of ordinary salt are strewn over a damp, evenly coloured area each salt kernel will soak up the dampness from its surroundings and with it the colour pigment. The result is a marvellous, but unpredictable, marbled or clouded effect. Different salts give different patterns, so it is best to experiment.

Watch point:
Be careful not to have any water standing on the fabric, or the salt will 'drown'.

Leave the salt on the silk until everything is dry, then brush it off with a soft brush and fix the paints as recommended by the manufacturer (see page 16).

Watch point:
The dryer the salt, the quicker it will work and the more moisture it can soak up.

Salt applied liberally to the fabric before the painting begins produces a well-defined pattern of dots.

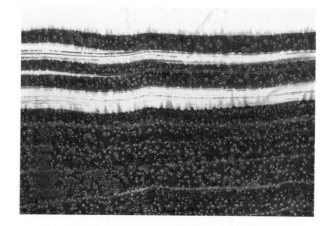

On a plain-coloured background, where very concentrated paint has been used, salt applied whilst the fabric is still wet will produce a marbled effect.

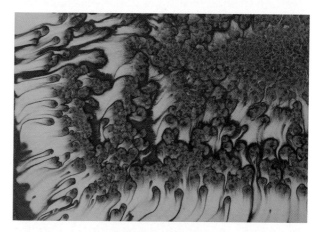

On a multi-coloured background of differing strengths of colour, salt applied while the fabric is still wet will produce unpredictable results.

Fixing

There are three principal ways of fixing silk paints: but whichever method you use, be sure to follow the manufacturer's instructions, and remember that you must never mix different makes of paint or fixatives.

1. Brushing on fixative

For some ranges manufacturers recommend a fixative in liquid form. It is brushed on after the paints are dry with a broad stiff brush. Work carefully and make sure that all of the silk fabric is well covered.

Watch point:
Work on a horizontal frame, otherwise some of the colours may run.

Leave to dry for one hour.
Take the fabric off the frame and handwash it in cold water. During the washing process some surplus dye may come out as well as any gutta used.
Hang up to dry; and, finally, iron. The colours should now be permanent and proved for hand-washing (30°C or 86°F) and dry-cleaning.

2. Ironing

Some water-based paints can be fixed by simply ironing with an electric iron set to the temperature recommended by the manufacturer. After the paints are dry take the silk off the frame. Make sure it does not touch anything wet or damp. Cover the ironing board with a clean piece of material and iron the silk all over from the 'wrong' side for 2-3 minutes. This will set the colours permanently for handwashing and dry-cleaning.

Watch point:
If the recommended ironing temperature is too hot for the fabric, protect it with a piece of paper between the iron and fabric.

3. Steaming

Alcohol-based silk paints are fixed by steaming.
There are on the market purpose-built steam ovens with detailed instructions, but they are rather too expensive for a beginner.

It is possible to steam small articles, however, like scarves, shawls, pictures, cushions or covers for lampshades, in a pressure-cooker, as follows. After the paints have dried for some hours, take the fabric off the frame and roll it very carefully into a larger piece of absorbent paper. Plain white blotting paper or wallpaper liner are ideal. The silk must lie absolutely flat, no pleats or wrinkles, and it must not overlap or touch itself. Roll the paper and silk into a sausage of about 1½ in (or 4 cm) diameter. Hold the roll closed with masking tape and also seal the ends.

Wrap roll loosely in aluminium foil. Semi-fold the parcel ends to allow steam to enter and to prevent condensation from running into the centre of the parcel so damaging the painted silk. Fill the pressure cooker with ¾ in (2 cm) of water or not quite to the base of the vegetable basket (see Fig a and b below). Fit the foil wrapped parcel into the basket without touching the sides, place the basket on the trivet inside the pressure cooker and close. Raise the pressure to 5lb per square inch and cook for about 45 minutes.

If no pressure cooker is available the steaming process can be done in a large pot with a well fitting lid, but the fixing time has to be trebled. Watch the water level – it should not be allowed to boil dry!

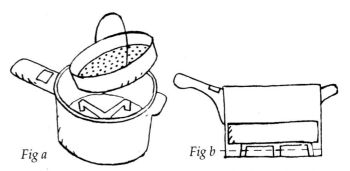

Fig a   *Fig b*

A domestic pressure-cooker may be used for fixing the paints by steaming. Fig a) shows the inside of the cooker; Fig b) shows the level of the water in the bottom of the cooker and the position of the foil-wrapped silk painting.

Instructions for pantograph

The following pages in this book give you various designs for ideas which you can copy. If you wish to use a design of your own choice and want it to stay the same size you can just trace it. You may, of course, wish to enlarge or reduce the actual drawings and there are several means by which you will be able to obtain an exact copy

There are various forms of photocopiers which will enlarge or reduce on paper. There are also more sophisticated machines which will copy a design to any size, on to any material but these can be rather costly.

The simplest way to reduce or enlarge is to use a pantograph which you can either make yourself or which you can obtain from most art and craft shops (see Fig a). A pantograph consists of four flattened rods or pieces of wood. At the appropriate points a tracing point is fixed to these rods for tracing the lines of the original and a drawing point for making the appropriate copy. The pantograph is hinged at the crossing points which can be adjusted to enlarge or reduce the copy.

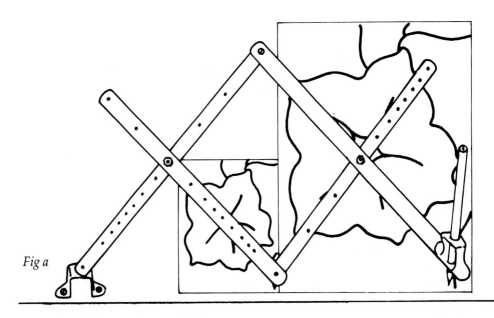

Fig a

Simple projects

Greetings cards

Who would not like to receive a hand-painted greetings card? Here is an opportunity for you to use gold and silver gutta without fear. Every silk painting technique is suitable. Pre-cut mounts are available in many sizes and they will give your silk paintings a professional finish.

Mounting a greetings card

A wide selection of ready-made mounts are available, complete with matching envelopes, but it is a simple matter to make your own mounts to any size. The card or paper you use will vary in price according to the quality and weight. Choose the colour of your mount very carefully, making sure it will enhance your silk painting.

You will also need sharp scissors, a ruler for trimming the card size and some glue. Rubber solution is recommended for most gluing, as it allows the picture to be repositioned if necessary.

Watch point:

If you are making your own mount, before finally deciding on the size of your card make sure you can obtain an envelope to match.

Cut a rectangle from the card and fold this in half. On the left-hand side – which will be the inside front of the card – mark an area large enough to take the silk painting, allowing about ½ in (1 cm) of the picture to be stuck down and leaving a margin of at least 1 in (2.5 cm) all round the card. Cut out this marked centre section, (Fig a).

With the right side of the silk painting facing you, lightly apply the glue as directed on the tube to the extreme edges. Place the painting face down on to the inside of the cut-out opening, making sure it is centrally positioned.

Once the glue is quite dry, fold the card in half so that the picture shows on the front and write your message on the inside.

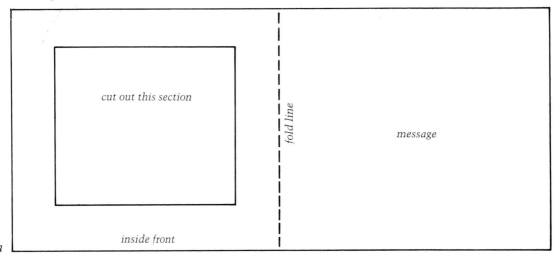

cut out this section

fold line

message

inside front

Fig a

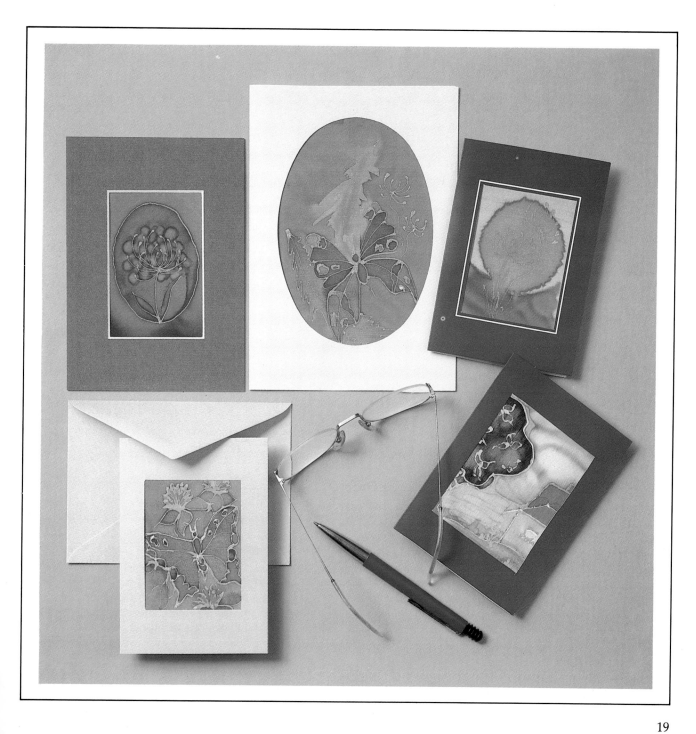

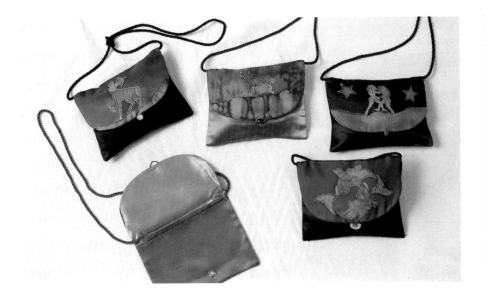

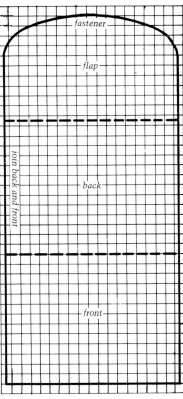

Fig b

Small bags or purses

Place the silk over a suitable drawing and copy the design with a soft pencil on to the silk. Frame up the silk as described on page 4 and apply gutta as indicated on page 11, following the pencil lines. Colour the small areas of the design with a fine brush, the larger background with a large brush using large even strokes. Fix the colours as recommended by the paint manufacturers.

Making a small purse

Use the pattern shown here, (Fig b), to cut out the completed silk painting and a separate piece of lining fabric. Each square on the pattern equals ¾ in (2 cm).

Join the side seams of the back and front on both pieces. With the wrong sides of each piece facing, insert the lining into the bag. Turn in both edges of the flap and neatly slip-stitch in place. Sew a press stud to the inside of the flap and the top of the front.

Brooches

These small colourful items are the ideal first projects. The colour combinations may be as wild and daring as you like, and, because the designs are so small, the shaky lines of an inexperienced hand will not be obvious. Also all stops and starts of a 'gutta' line can be outside the design, so that they will not show, because they are folded around to the back.

Cover a small card disc with the silk. To give it more body, pad it with some foam rubber which is cut to the size of the cardboard disc. Fold the surplus fabric to the back. Either stick it down or sew it up. Cover the back of the brooch with another cardboard disc, which has a safety pin attached to it.

Silk cushions

Luxurious cushions are practical yet ornamental furnishings and need not be expensive. The beauty of your own original silk cushions will add the finishing touch to any room and highlight a colour scheme. Even if you are not an experienced needlewoman, cushion making presents few problems.

First determine the size of the cushion you intend to make–18 in (46 cm) square is a popular size. For the cover you will need to buy sufficient silk for the painted front of the cushion and a similar amount for the plain back. As a guide, a length of 20 in (51 cm) from a 40 in (102 cm) wide fabric should be enough to cover an 18 in (46 cm) cushion. This will allow about 1 in (2.5 cm) all round for seaming.

Ready-made pads to fit inside the cushion cover are available in different sizes and shapes from most furnishing departments and stores. Inexpensive pads are usually filled with kapok, or a mixture of down and feathers.

Making a cushion cover

Place the completed silk painting and the remaining piece of silk together, with the right sides facing each other. Tack along three of the sides of the square, about ½ in (1 cm) in from the edge. Insert the cushion pad very gently and check that it will fit snugly–if not, re-tack the seams.

Seam these three edges by machine, or by hand using small, neat back-stitches. Unpick the tacking stitches.

Watch point:
To give a perfect fit at the corners, the seams of the cover should now be squared off. This will ensure that

there are no unsightly lumps of fabric. Before closing the remaining seam trim each corner diagonally across, (Fig a). Take care not to cut too close to the stitches.

Turn the cover right side out and insert the cushion pad. To close the remaining opening, turn ½ in (1 cm) along both edges to the inside and slip-stitch them together, keeping the stitches small and neat so that they barely show.

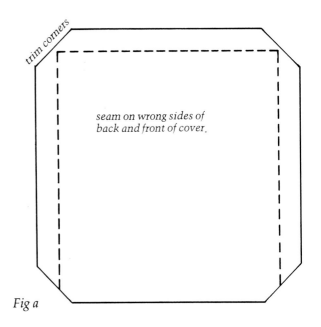

trim corners

seam on wrong sides of back and front of cover.

Fig a

Opposite: the design was drawn with gutta on to the stretched silk and left to dry. The fabric was then brushed with thinner and diagonal stripes were painted on to the wet fabric.

Above: three cushions showing, left, the watercolour technique; middle, gutta technique and right, salt technique.

Opposite: two cushions showing the use of gold gutta. On the left, the leaves were sprinkled with salt while still wet and, right, salt was sprinkled along the branches.

Silk pictures

Painting on silk is the ideal way of creating an original masterpiece, combining unique shapes and blends of colours. Choose a subject which will add to the atmosphere of a room–strong and bold for a living area; soft and subtle for a bedroom.

When the painting is completed, it will need to be mounted and framed. Most art shops will undertake this whole process for you but if you want to try this stage for yourself, you can also obtain the necessary materials and equipment from the same source.

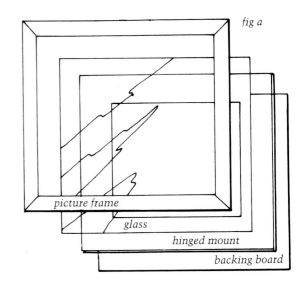

fig a

picture frame

glass

hinged mount

backing board

Picture frames

The illustration (Fig a) shows the components that go to make up the mount, back and frame. Either purchase a frame which includes all these accessories, or assemble them separately–old frames can be picked up very cheaply at jumble sales but the backing and mounting materials will need replacing.

Plain backing

Glazed frames require a firm backing to hold the picture rigid and to keep out dust. The most suitable material is hardboard but some frame mouldings are rather shallow and will not take the thickness of the hardboard. A thin, strong cardboard makes an effective alternative.

Decorative front mount

The silk painting will not extend to the full area of the material because it has to be pinned out on a frame. The unpainted edges will therefore need to be concealed by a cardboard surround. White, or coloured mounting boards are available at most art shops. Select a colour which will complement the painting, without clashing with the decor of the room.

Opposite: willow in summer, above, combines watercolour and salt techniques. The background was painted wet on wet and the centres of the foliage sprinkled with salt and left to dry slowly.
Willows in autumn, below, was painted in the watercolour technique. When completely dry, the willows were added with thickened paint.

Mounting and framing

Cut a piece of decorative mounting card to the inner measurements of the frame and allow an additional ¼ in (6 mm) all round to fit into the frame rebate. Cut a backing mount to exactly the same size.

Check the area of the painting that needs to be concealed by the decorative mount and pencil in a 'window'. Ensure that this gives a well-balanced sight area of the picture. Use a steel rule and a sharp craft knife to cut out the window, (Fig b).

To complete the mount, join the top edge of the decorative front and the backing together with strong sticky tape. Position the painting on the backing so that the desired area is seen through the window on the front. Use four strips of double-sided sticky tape to attach the picture to the backing at each corner, (Fig c).

Place the mounted picture in the frame face downwards. Pin the hardboard back in place with panel pins, lightly tapped into the inner edges of the frame. Attach picture hooks and cord, or picture wire if the frame is heavy.

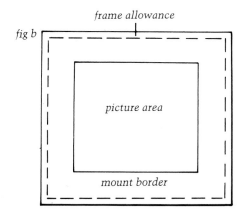

fig b

frame allowance

picture area

mount border

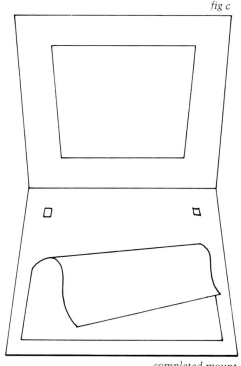

fig c

completed mount

Opposite: the background for this butterfly picture was painted and left to dry. The outlines of the butterfly were drawn with transparent gutta and left to dry. The wings were coloured in and some areas were treated with salt when wet, some had water sprinkled on when dry. The body had water stripes painted in when the background was almost dry.
Finally, the dark brown outer edge was painted in and left to bleed into the background.

Above and front cover: this painting shows the use of gold gutta, with watercolour and salt techniques, to superb effect. The outlines require very little artistic skill.

Above : these cottages were painted in watercolour, apart from the door and window frames. To keep these white, they were first drawn in with gutta and left to dry. The edges outlining different areas appear when wet paint is applied to a dry background.

Silk scarves

The projects given in this book so far have all had their raw edges concealed by mounting or seaming methods. The edges of a scarf, however, remain visible and they must be finished off very neatly.

A silk scarf with an original design in luminous colours deserves to be finished in the best way. Straight, machine hemming is possible; it is quick but not really worthy of a luxury article. A rolled hem gives the neatest result and can be worked in one of two ways; either by machine and hand, or entirely by machine using a narrow hemmer foot.

Hand-rolled hem

Make sure all the edges of the silk are perfectly straight. Allow a total of ½ in (1 cm) around all edges for the finished rolled hem. Work a staystitch with small machine stitches ⅛ in (3 mm) from the raw edges. Trim the fabric away to within a few threads of the machining. (Fig a).

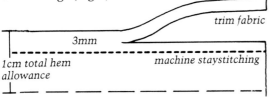

Fig a

Turn the full hem allowance to the wrong side and roll the raw edge under so that the line of machine stitching just shows. Thread a fine sewing needle with the same thread and work from right to left along the hem. Sew along the hem with small, loose blind stitches–these are similar to slip-stitches–working through the machine stitching and edge of the scarf.

Make several stitches and then gently pull up the slack in the thread. This will cause the edge to roll under, (Fig b).

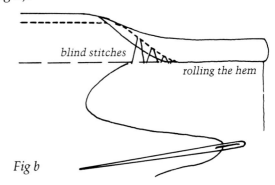

Fig b

Machine-rolled hem

Trim the edge to allow ¼ in (6 mm) hem. To hold the hem in place, gently press along the foldline with your fingers. Turn the same edge under again to form a double hem and press with your fingers in the same way.

Slip the double hem into place under the hemmer foot and stitch in place, (Fig c).

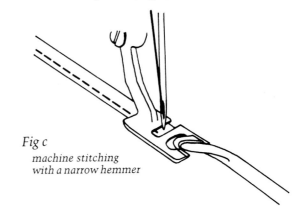

Fig c
machine stitching with a narrow hemmer

Above: the whole scarf was worked in gutta, or resist method, using transparent gutta, red and blue paints, and mixtures of these. Colours from the same manufacturer can be mixed, but it is not advisable to mix paints of different makes.

Above: this scarf shows a posy of delicate alpine flowers balanced by very strong geometric bands on two sides, picking up the same colours used for the flowers. Gutta and watercolour techniques are used. This design was taken from the motif on page 47.

Above: this scarf shows a variation of the alpine theme on the opposite page, with the design drawn in gutta. The blossom is painted in the watercolour technique in rose, brown and grey and the stripes repeat these colours.

Above: the bloom of the poppy provides inspiration for this scarf. The design is drawn with gold gutta, with the stamens also in gold.

Above: the three silk painting techniques are combined to produce the striking design for this scarf, using beige, rust and black.

Above: a completely abstract drawing with very fine gutta lines has been used for the design on this scarf. Within the outlines, soft hues of beige, pink, coral and red have been applied by the watercolour technique.

Above: the clever use of letters of the alphabet produces the design for this brightly-coloured scarf. A steady hand is needed to draw the straight lines with gutta.

Fashion

When you make a garment from pure silk that has also been hand-painted, you are entering the world of haute couture. Having perfected your skill at painting on silk, you must also have some basic knowledge of dressmaking to undertake the projects shown in this section. The following hints will also be useful in producing perfect results.

Delicate fabrics need careful treatment to obtain the best results, so use fine pins, needles and thread, and special finishes for seams and hems.

Try not to handle the material too much and keep the number of rows of machining to an absolute minimum–this avoids the risk of marking or puckering the fabric.

The choice of style for a silk garment is of prime importance. It should be soft and flowing with gathers and unpressed pleats, rather than a figure-hugging shape. Select patterns with the minimum of seaming and try to avoid those which require facings, as these will show through as ridges on the garment.

Seams and hems must not be too bulky. An overedge seam is the simplest method but care must be taken not to work the zigzag stitches too tightly, or the seam will be drawn up and the garment will not hang correctly. Use a mock French seam in place of the normal version, as this is easier to control when machining round curves. There is also less risk of puckering the fabric with this method, as the first stage produces the seam that shows on the right side of the garment. A self-bound seam gives a very neat finish and is suitable for straight or curved seams.

Silk with its luxurious softness and sheen has always been a favourite in high fashion. Now it is up to you to combine the fabric with stunning designs and daring colour schemes to create original garments of striking elegance! Choose a dress of simple cut which will show your painting to its best advantage. Make sure that the design fits well into the shape of the individual garment pieces. It may help to have the outlines of the garment pieces marked on the silk with a soft pencil before starting to paint, but do not forget that an initial seam allowance is needed of at least ½ in (1 cm).

Overedge seam

With the right sides of the pieces facing each other, machine along the seamline. Gently press both seam allowances flat towards the back of the garment. Trim both allowances to ¼ in (6 mm).

Use close, short machine zigzag stitches to join the raw edges together, or overcast the edges by hand, (Fig a).

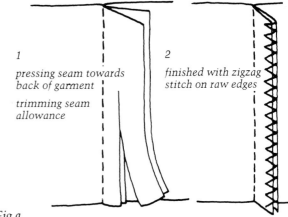

1
pressing seam towards back of garment

trimming seam allowance

2
finished with zigzag stitch on raw edges

Fig a

Mock French seam

With the right sides of the pieces facing each other, machine along the seamline. Gently press both seam allowances flat towards the back of the garment.

Fold the raw edges of both pieces ⅛ in (3 mm) in to face each other. Finger press together, (see page 32), and pin close to the folded edges. Machine along this edge to complete the seam, (Fig b).

Self-bound seam

With the right sides of the pieces facing each other, machine along the seamline. Gently press both seam allowances flat towards the back of the garment. Trim the seam allowance closest to the garment to ⅛ in (3 mm), and use the other allowance to bind them both together.

Turn under ⅛ in (3 mm) of the untrimmed seam allowance to the seamline, enclosing the trimmed edge. Machine stitch or hand sew, keeping just above the previous line of machining, (Fig c).

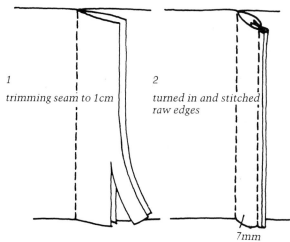

1
trimming seam to 1cm

2
turned in and stitched raw edges

7mm

Fig b

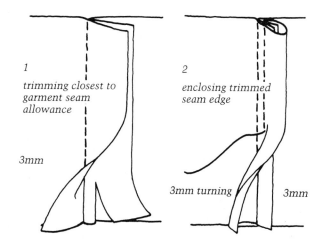

1
trimming closest to garment seam allowance

3mm

2
enclosing trimmed seam edge

3mm turning   3mm

Fig c

Above: the very straight cut and simple striped pattern of the evening dress is in strong contrast to the softly-draped butterfly stole.

Above: the loose fitting blouse, demonstrates that uncomplicated shapes are more suitable for garments made of hand-painted silk, as they show the design and colour scheme to their best advantage.

Above: the shape of this elegant chemise and the simple motif, make it the ideal choice for your first venture into the field of fashion, as it requires the minimum of painting and dress-making skills.
On a natural cream background, draw basic blossom shapes on the front and back sections of the chemise with colourless gutta. When the gutta has completely dried, colour the whole surface of the fabric, using a sponge to apply the paint evenly.

Opposite: for this jacket with raglan sleeves the design of overlapping leaves is kept to the main areas of the garment pattern pieces, back, sleeve and collar, so that it will not interfere with the making up of the jacket.
The design is drawn in transparent gutta on to natural coloured silk, coloured in with undiluted deep green and turquoise. The background is painted with diluted blue. The jacket is lined with a dark blue silk and interlined with synthetic wadding.

The fabric is painted in the gutta technique, and the design is kept to the main panels of the garment pattern. Note how the design is adapted so as not to interfere with the centre back seam of the collar or the seams of the raglan sleeves. Enlarge the drawing below to the size required to fit into the area of fabric on the back of the jacket. You can add further gutta lines by hand to complete the design.

Motifs for silk painting

Enlarge this drawing for the alpine flowers shown on the scarf on page 34.

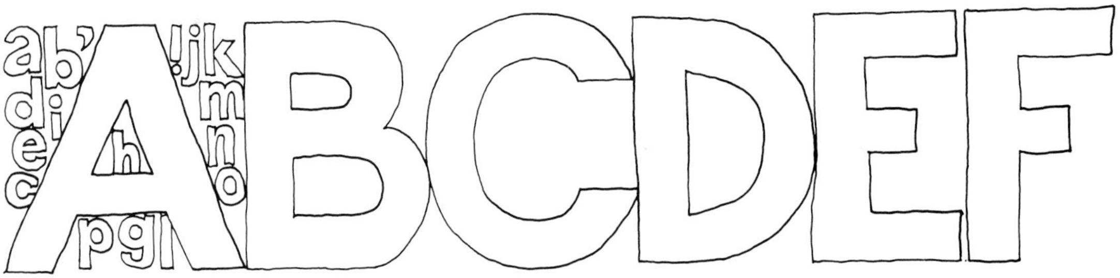
ABCDEF

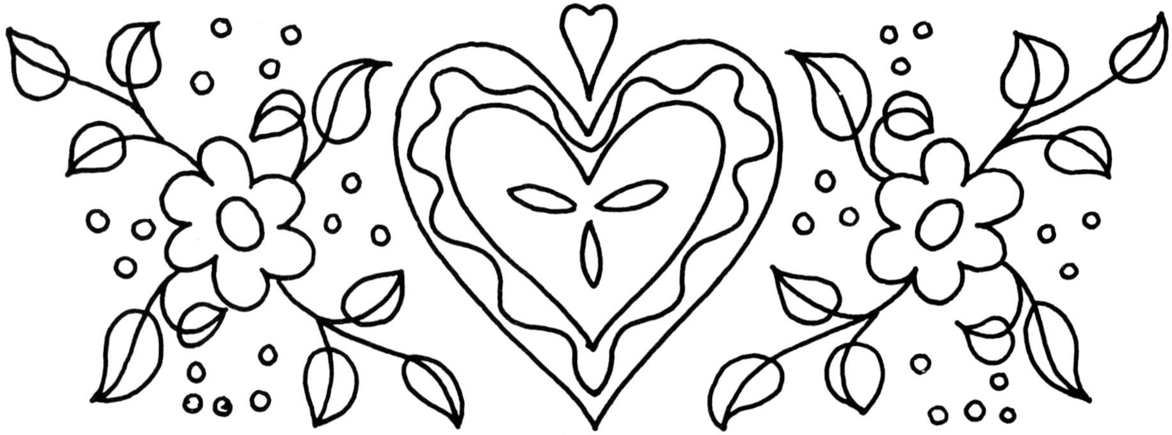

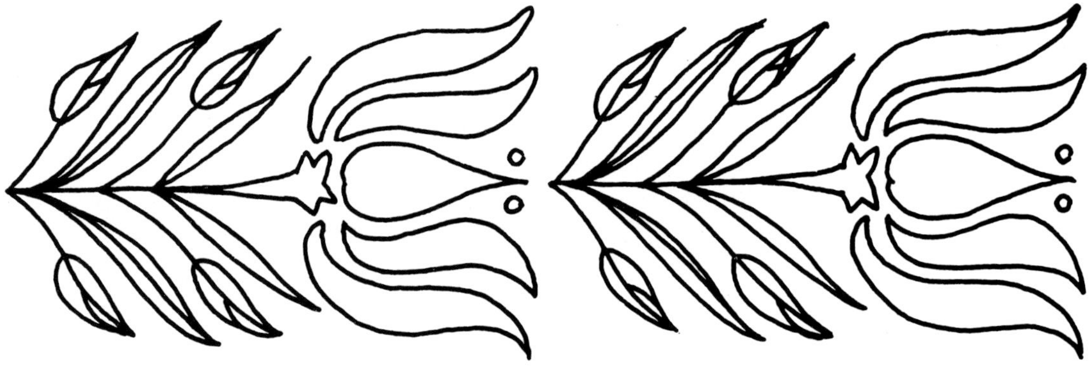